This time Julius Alvin has gone TOO far!

An eighty-year-old man told his family he was going to marry a woman much younger than he was. His son said to him. "Do you realize that marrying a woman of eighteen could be fatal?"

The old man considered the problem briefly then said, "Well, if she dies, she dies."

Did you hear about the stripper who couldn't retire?

Whenever she saw tip money on a restaurant table she'd get up and dance.

What is poetic justice?

When your brother-in-law who never smokes, drinks, or swears gets gonorrhea.

What did Pee Wee Herman say to Madonna?

"Damn! When *I* did that I got arrested!"

Have you heard about the new Ronald Reagan computer?

It has no memory and no colon.

DISGUSTINGLY FUNNY!
THESE ARE DEFINITELY NOT THE JOKES
YOU'D WANT TO TELL YOUR MOTHER!

GROSS JOKES

By JULIUS ALVIN

AGONIZINGLY GROSS JOKES	(3648-5, $3.50/$4.50)
AWESOMELY GROSS JOKES	(3613-2, $3.50/$4.50)
DOUBLY GROSS JOKES	(3980-8, $3.50/$4.50)
EXCRUCIATINGLY GROSS JOKES	(3289-7, $3.50/$4.50)
EXTREMELY GROSS JOKES	(3678-7, $3.50/$4.50)
FRESH GROSS JOKES	(3981-6, $3.50/$4.50)
GROSS JOKES	(3620-5, $3.50/$4.50)
PAINFULLY GROSS JOKES	(3621-3, $3.50/$4.50)
RUDE GROSS JOKES	(3616-7, $3.50/$4.50)
TOTALLY GROSS JOKES	(3622-1, $3.50/$4.50)
UTTERLY GROSS JOKES	(3982-4, $3.50/$4.50)

Available wherever paperbacks are sold, or order direct from the Publisher. Send cover price plus 50¢ per copy for mailing and handling to Penguin USA, P.O. Box 999, c/o Dept. 17109, Bergenfield, NJ 07621. Residents of New York and Tennessee must include sales tax. DO NOT SEND CASH.

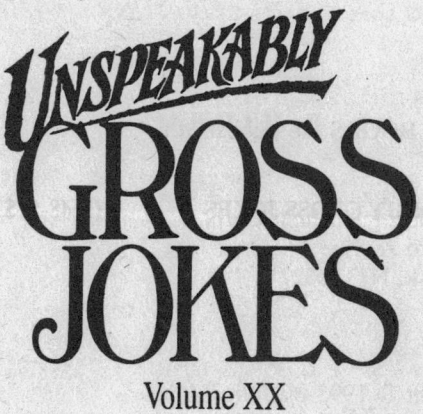

Volume XX

by Julius Alvin

ZEBRA BOOKS
KENSINGTON PUBLISHING CORP.

ZEBRA BOOKS are published by

Kensington Publishing Corp.
850 Third Avenue
New York, NY 10022

Copyright © 1995 by Julius Alvin

All rights reserved. No part of this book may be reproduced in any form or by any means without the prior written consent of the Publisher, excepting brief quotes used in reviews.

If you purchased this book without a cover, you should be aware that this book is stolen property. It was reported as "unsold and destroyed" to the Publisher and neither the Author nor the Publisher has received any payment for this "stripped book."

Zebra and the Z logo Reg. U.S. Pat. & TM Off.

First Printing: July, 1995

Printed in the United States of America

TABLE OF CONTENTS

Chapter One: Men & Women	7
Chapter Two: Heterosexuals	17
Chapter Three: Homosexuals	35
Chapter Four: Celebrities	43
Chapter Five: Rednecks	51
Chapter Six: Pros & Hobbyists	57
Chapter Seven: Gross Elephant Jokes	71
Chapter Eight: Gross Gerbil Jokes	79
Chapter Nine: Gross Animal Jokes	85
Chapter Ten: SPECIAL FEATURE: Handy Bragging Tips	95
Chapter Eleven: Boogers, Farts, & More	101
Chapter Twelve: Watch Your Fucking Language	119
Chapter Thirteen: SPECIAL FEATURE: Movie Ratings	131
Chapter Fourteen: AIDS Jokes	133
Chapter Fifteen: Somalia	137
Chapter Sixteen: Shitty Jokes	143
Chapter Seventeen: Tongue Twisters	147
Chapter Eighteen: Sexual Specialties	151

Chapter One:

Men & Women

Did you hear about the guy whose buddies called him Scrotum?

He was something between a prick and an asshole.

Did you hear about the woman who had too many face-lifts?

She had nipples on her face.

Shannon (five years old): Mommy, where do babies come from?

Mommy: Well, sperm from Daddy fertilizes the egg from Mommy, and the baby grows in Mommy's tummy.

Shannon: How does the sperm from Daddy get into Mommy? Does she swallow it?

Mommy: If she wants a new diamond, she does.

How can you make a man stop biting his nails?

Knock his teeth out.

Did you hear about the dwarf who got fired by his female boss?

She said he was always getting in her hair.

Why don't single women fart?

Because they don't have assholes until they get married.

Why do brides smile so much on their wedding day?

Because they know they've given their last blow jobs.

Therapist: Mr. Fogarty, how long has it been since you've had sex?

Mr. Fogarty: About four inches long.

Did you hear about the actress who became a porn star?

It was due to her oral presentation.

Why do Italian men wear moustaches?

So they look like their mothers.

How can you tell when a stuck-up bitch has an orgasm?

She drops her nail file.

Once, little Jason wandered into his parents' room when his father was buck naked. Staring at his father's privates, he asked, "Daddy, what's that?"

Jason's father proudly told him, "That's my penis. In fact, it's the perfect penis." Jason's curiosity was satisfied.

The next day, Jason was walking to school with little Michelle, and he said, "C'mere. I wanna show you something." In the bushes, Jason dropped his pants and showed Michelle his pecker.

"What's that?" asked Michelle.

"That's my penis," said Jason. "In fact, if it were two inches shorter, it'd be the perfect penis."

Why do WASP women have so many wrinkles on their faces?

From squinting and saying, "Suck what?"

I know a girl who lives on a hill,
She won't fool around but her sister will.
I know a guy from Niagara Falls,
The crabs run races on his balls.
I know a girl named Buffalo Jill,
She won't fool around but her buffalo will.
I know a fag, his name is Bruce,
He blows his wad when the juice is loose.
I know a girl in Lackawanna,
She knows how but she don't wanna.
I know an Italian, his name is Tony,
Even his shit smells like pepperoni.

What is menstruation?

A bloody waste of fucking time.

What do you call twenty-four women in a box?

A case of slits.

Why did the woman get fired from her modeling job at the auto show?

She was showing all her options.

Did you hear about the woman who almost gagged on her doctor's tongue depressor?

She was okay after he zipped it up again.

Why didn't the hooker want to try butt-fucking?

She thought a half-inch cigarette couldn't feel good.

Police Officer (during raid): This is a bust!

Hooker: Thank you for noticing.

Employer (during interview): Do you have a union card?

Bimbo: I didn't know I had to have a *card* to do it.

When God was creating people, he decided to make four groups: White, Black, Oriental, and Middle Eastern. He told them that each group would get one special request. The Middle Eastern people said, "We want to be great warriors."

God said, "Bam! There you are."

The Orientals said, "We want great wisdom."

God said, "Bam! There you are."

The Whites said, "We want to be filthy rich."

When the Blacks heard that, they said, "Great! Well, you can suck our big dicks!"

So God gave them big dicks.

Chapter Two:

Heterosexuals

Did you hear about the girl who went fishing with twelve guys?

She came back with a red snapper.

Did you hear about the horny Chinese restaurant owner who asked his wife for a little sixty-nine?

She said, "Cook it yourself."

Did you hear about the woman who had a talking cunt?

It was her answering cervix.

An eighty-year-old man told his family he was going to marry a woman much younger than he was. His son said to him, "Do you realize that marrying a woman of eighteen could be fatal?"

The old man considered the problem briefly, then said, "Well, if she dies, she dies."

How do we know that God wants men to eat pussy?

Because he made it look like a taco.

What's the dirtiest cook book ever written?

How to Work Wonders with One Pound of Meat.

What's the difference between a sixteen-year-old girl and a bowling ball?

You can get three fingers into a bowling ball.

What goes in hard and comes out soft and sticky?

Bubblegum.

An elderly couple on a fixed income was having trouble making ends meet. "Mabel," said Dewey, "I'm afraid there's only one thing we can do. You must sell your body on the street."

"If that's what must be done," said Mabel, "then, God forgive me, I'll do it."

That evening, Mabel went out on the town. Dewey sat up until nine A.M. the next morning, when Mabel finally dragged herself in the door.

"How did you do?"

"I made five dollars and ten cents."

Dewey was aghast. "You've been out all night and you only got five dollars and ten cents?! Who in the hell gave you ten cents?"

"Everybody."

UNSPEAKABLY GROSS JOKES

What's six inches long, has a head on it, and drives women wild?

A hundred dollar bill.

What's the string on a tampon for?

So you can floss after you eat.

Why are black men always playing with their dicks?

That's the only thing the white men have left them.

Did you hear about the woman who was hungry for knowledge?

She ate a professor for lunch.

What should you do if you receive obscene mail?

Report him to an obscene female.

Three guys were out on a cruise when the ship suddenly began to sink.
The first guy yelled, "Women and children first!"
The second guy shouted, "Fuck the women and children!"
The third guy said, "Do we have the time?"

Why did the moron give up masturbating?

It got out of hand.

What is poetic justice?

When your brother-in-law who never smokes, drinks, or swears gets gonorrhea.

Did you hear about the man who was born with a corkscrew-shaped cock?

He searched all his life for a woman with a corkscrew-shaped cunt-hole, and when he was seventy-eight years old he finally found her . . . but the damned woman had a left-handed threading!

Why did Mike Tyson always buy his date dinner?

Because the rest of the night was on her.

What do peanut butter and a slut have in common?

Both have been spread and eaten by just about everyone.

What's the best line to use to pick up a soldier?

"Hey, baby, how do you like *this* foxhole?"

UNSPEAKABLY GROSS JOKES

What's immaculate conception?

Having an alcohol rubdown just before sex.

What's a premature ejaculator?

A nine-year-old boy.

What's the difference between a gemstone and a slut?

Gemstones aren't cheap.

A tiny, frail old man went into a whorehouse and asked for a girl. He was shown to a small room. When the girl came in, the little old man said to her, "Hold it, I gotta go to the bathroom."

When he came out of the bathroom, he had cotton balls stuffed in his ears and nose. "Okay, let's go," he said.

"Wait a minute," said the hooker. "What's all the cotton for?"

The old man smiled and said, "There's two things I can't stand: the sound of screaming women and the smell of burning rubber!"

How do we know that Adam was the first soft-drink manufacturer?

He made Eve's cherry pop.

How do we know that Eve was the first carpenter?

She made Adam's banana stand.

What's the difference between a paper clip and a screw?

I don't know . . . I've never been paper clipped.

What do you get when you cross an apple with a stuck-up bitch?

A computer that won't go down.

A fireman told his wife that he was going to run their house like a fire station. "If one bell goes off, you run in the bedroom. If two bells go off, you take off your clothes. If three bells go off, you get in bed."

Later that night, she heard one bell and ran to the bedroom. Then she heard two bells and took off her clothes. Then she heard three bells and got in bed. Then she started ringing the bell.

"Wait a minute," he cried. "There ain't no four bells!"

"Yes there is— you need more hose or you ain't gettin' to the fire!"

Why did the woman throw away her vibrator?

It kept chipping her teeth.

Did you hear about the college professor who was fucking his female students?

He ended up with a couple of dilated pupils.

Friends may come and friends may go,
And friends may peter out, you know;
But we'll be friends through thick and thin,
Peter out or peter in.

What do you call a quickie in the snow?

A coolie.

Did you hear about the stripper who couldn't retire?

Whenever she saw tip money on a restaurant table, she'd get up and dance.

———————

Three guys were bragging about how they could make their wives hot. The first guy said, "I kiss her body all over, and I mean all over. It gets her hot."
The second guy said, "I put whipped cream all over her body; then I lick it all off. That makes her real hot."
The third guy said, "I've got both you guys beat. I slap her, knock her down to the floor, fuck the shit out of her, then wipe my dick off on the curtains."

What did the old lady say when her old husband had his first erection in thirteen years?

"Now that you've got the wrinkles out, this might be a good time to wash it."

Why did the man get all dressed up for his vasectomy?

He said, "If I'm gonna *be* impotent, I want to *look* impotent."

Why did the woman kiss her husband good night on his pecker?

Because his breath was terrible.

Have you heard about the new X-rated cartoon remake?

It's called "Betty Shtoop."

What's sixty-eight?

"You suck me and I'll owe you one."

Two guys, Hollis and Bill, were bragging about their sexual proclivities. Hollis was making such impossible claims as to his own virility that Bill had to challenge him. "If you can fuck a hundred women in an hour, then I'll not only concede that you're the best, but I'll give you a thousand dollars."

Hollis confidently agreed, and the two men set a date for the great event.

When the day finally arrived, there were one hundred women on one hundred beds ready to participate in the challenge.

Hollis arrived, announcing that he was ready to perform. When the timekeeper signaled, Hollis started to fuck. He was doing great. After half an hour, he had done sixty women. He started running into a little trouble though; after forty minutes, he was only up to sixty-eight. When the time ran out, he had only fucked seventy-three women.

Bill said, "You know, it looked like you were gonna make it. What happened?"

"I don't know," said Hollis. "It went all right at practice this morning."

Chapter Three:

Homosexuals

Why did the gay sailor quit the navy?

He found out what a frigate really was.

What did the gay man say when the arresting officer asked him who his partner was?

"Do you think I've got eyes in the back of my head?"

How do you pick up a gay man at a bar?

"May I push in your stool?"

How can you tell that Superman was gay?

Because he got into Clark Kent's pants every morning.

Did you hear about the gay whale?

He went up to a submarine, bit off its tail, and sucked out the seamen.

I'm gonna beat my meat on a toilet seat,
Bang my twang with the rest of the gang,
Stroke my yoke before I smoke,
Yank my crank and then call Frank.

What new movie are Sylvester Stallone and Barney Frank doing?

Rambutt.

Why don't congressmen like bookmarks?

They prefer bending over pages.

What do you call a southern gay man?

A homo-suck-y'all.

Why should you be gay if you want to be a dentist?

Sooner or later, you're going to have to put your tool in another man's mouth.

What's a speed bump?

A hemorrhoid on a fag.

He was a harmless gay guy who wouldn't bother a fly . . . unless it was open.

What's a lesbian's favorite pickup line?

"Your face or mine?"

What do you call photos of famous lesbians?

Memora-labia.

Two homosexuals were talking about heaven and hell. The first one said, "I don't believe any of that stuff, but if I did, I'd sure wanna go to heaven when I died."

The second one said, "I don't believe any of it either, but if I had a choice, I'd wanna go to hell."

"For Pete's sake, why?"

" 'Cause I wanna meet Liberace!"

Did you hear about the new gay sitcom?

It's called "Leave It, It's Beaver."

What do anal sex and filet mignon have in common?

Raw meat.

Why are there so many gays in San Francisco?

Half of them were born there, and the other half were sucked into it.

Two queers were out driving when they got into a fender-bender with a pickup truck. The gay driver began to apologize, but the driver of the pickup was furious. "Fuck you!" he yelled at the two men.
The gay man said to his buddy, "Go ahead, he wants to settle out of court!"

What do you call the bouncer at a gay bar?

A flame thrower.

Why don't gays whisper in each other's ears?

They don't want to get hearing AIDS.

How many men can you get into a gay limousine?

Seventy-seven. You can get eight in the front and sixty-nine in the rear.

A gay man went into a deli and asked for a stick of salami. The butcher asked, "Would you like that sliced?"
The man said, "Does my ass look like a piggy bank?"

Three gay men were in the tub together when some semen rose to the surface. The three guys looked at each other for a moment. One of them finally said, "All right, who farted?"

First, there was Tom, Dick, 'n' Harry. Then Harry said, "Tom, cut that out!"

Chapter Four:

Celebrities

Why did Pee Wee Herman decide to be his own lawyer?

He said he could get himself off.

Why didn't Pee Wee Herman get convicted?

The evidence wouldn't stand up in court.

What did Pee Wee Herman say to Madonna?

"Damn! When *I* did that I got arrested!"

Have you heard about Pee Wee Herman's new TV show?

It's called "Captain Yankeroo."

What's the difference between Pee Wee Herman and Jeffrey Dahmer?

Pee Wee beats it; Jeffrey eats it.

UNSPEAKABLY GROSS JOKES

What did Jeffrey Dahmer say to Pee Wee Herman?

"Get your hands off my lunch!"

What goes into thirteen twice?

Woody Allen.

What's Woody Allen's new movie?

Close Encounters with the Third Grade.

Why did Salvador Dali paint a clock draped like a leaf over a tree?

He was impotent.

What were Joan of Arc's last words?

"Is it me, or is it really hot in here?"

What were Socrates' last words?

"I drank what?"

What were Ted Bundy's last words?

"Ouch!"

Why were the guards at Joan of Arc's execution so upset?

They didn't have any barbeque sauce.

What was the last thing John Wilkes Booth said before he shot Lincoln?

"For the last time—take that damn hat off!"

What did the narcotics agents find under Roseanne Barr's dress?

Fifty pounds of crack.

Did you hear that someone is suing Dr. Jack Kevorkian for malpractice?

He saved their life.

Have you heard about the new Ronald Reagan computer?

It has no memory and no colon.

Why did Helen Keller masturbate with only one hand?

She used the other hand to moan.

UNSPEAKABLY GROSS JOKES

Why did Helen Keller have yellow socks?

Her dog was blind, too.

How does Sinead O'Connor part her hair?

She squats.

What did the authorities find when they removed Tammy Faye Bakker's makeup?

Jimmy Hoffa.

What do you call Barbra Streisand's pubic hair?

Yentl floss.

What do you get when you dynamite Barney the Dinosaur?

Barney Rubble.

Chapter Five:

Rednecks

Why do rednecks like to eat lamb?

It reminds them of their first date.

Why do so many rednecks have two names, like Billy Bob or Bubba Ray?

Because they're named after their daddies.

Why don't rednecks ever get false teeth?

They would interfere with spitting.

How can you tell if a redneck is level-headed?

He has tobacco juice running down both sides of his chin.

How does a redneck know he had a good time at the party last night?

He wakes up in a pool of his own vomit.

How does a redneck describe a woman's sexual maturity?

"After eight, it's too late."

What's a redneck virgin?

An eight-year-old who can run faster than her brothers.

What's redneck foreplay?

"Get in the truck, bitch."

What's a redneck's idea of the best place to pick up girls?

The daycare center.

How does a redneck introduce his wife?

"This is my wife and sister, Marybelle."

What does a redneck say after he has sex?

"Thanks, Ma."

UNSPEAKABLY GROSS JOKES

Gomer: Have you heard about the new sexual position?
Jethro: No.
Gomer: First, you put on a pair of rubber boots. Then you take your sheep to the top of a cliff, face her out over the edge, and pump away. It's great— the sheep'll push back on you to keep from goin' over the edge.
Jethro: Okay, but what are the rubber boots for?
Gomer: You stick the sheep's hind legs in 'em, and they keep her from running away.

What do rednecks use for fishing lures?

Tapeworms.

How does a redneck know when he has reached adulthood?

His last tooth falls out.

This here's the story 'bout a man named Jed.
The dumbshit never wore a rubber on his head.
Then one day he was screwing Elly May,
And up from his nuts came a bubble and a spray.
>   White gold. Texas pee.

Well, the next thing you know, old Jed's on the run.
Granny's chasing him with a big shotgun.
She said, "In jail is where you ought to be."
So he loaded up the truck and he fled the county.
>   Out of the hills, that is.

Chapter Six:

Pros & Hobbyists

How do you insult a flasher?

"Hey, that looks exactly like a penis . . . only smaller!"

Did you hear about the flasher who was going to retire?

He changed his mind and decided to stick it out a bit longer.

How can you tell if a model is a nymphomaniac?

She has sex the same day she has her hair done.

———————

Why did the flight attendant get fired?

She kept going up to the passengers, pointing to her crotch, and saying, "Put *this* over your mouth and nose and breathe normally."

———————

Why do chefs have rubber scrapers?

So they can reuse those little things.

———————

Did you hear about the dentist who ran a thriving practice?

He was filling some unusual cavities.

Did you hear about the crack furniture salesman?

He sold beds.

Why did the Puerto Rican get run over?

Someone was trying to save money on car grease.

What is San Francisco doing about the infestation of Mcdflies?

They've established the Fruit Police.

Have you heard about the new Oriental cook book?

It's called *101 Ways to Wok Your Dog*.

What's the difference between General Motors corporate headquarters and a cactus?

A cactus has the pricks on the outside.

Don wasn't too cautious when it came to having safe sex. Pretty soon he got the clap. When his penis became swollen, Don panicked. He ran into the doctor's office and, in front of all the other patients, yelled out, "Help, Doc! There's something wrong with my prick!"

The doctor took him aside and said, "If you have to shout about it in my waiting room, call it your arm." Then he examined Don, gave him some clap medicine, and told him to be back on Wednesday morning.

On Wednesday morning the doctor's office was full of patients. When the doc saw Don come in, he called out, "Hi, Don! How's your arm this morning?"

"Dammit, doc," said Don, "it's so sore I can't even piss through it!"

Did you hear about the macho aerobics instructor?

He got a vasectomy and jogged home.

What does a French-Chinese prostitute do?

She sucks your laundry.

Why was the master chef so sad?

He let his meat loaf.

What do you get when you cross a hooker and a computer?

A fucking know-it-all.

———————

What do you get when you cross a black, an Eskimo, and a hooker?

A snowblower that doesn't work.

———————

What do you get when you cross a Cabbage Patch doll with the Pillsbury Doughboy?

An ugly fat broad with a yeast infection.

———————

A theater owner once told me:
"The new cinematic emporium
Is not just a super sensorium,
But a highly effectual, heterosexual,
Mutual masturbatorium."

―――――――

Why are lefties such great lovers?

They do it right.

―――――――

Why are hunters such great lovers?

They are always loaded.

―――――――

UNSPEAKABLY GROSS JOKES

Why are biologists such great lovers?

They have multiple organisms.

Why are truckers such great lovers?

They deliver.

Why are jugglers such great lovers?

They do it with their balls in the air.

Why are seismologists such great lovers?

They register on the Richter scale.

Why are cooks such great lovers?

They have better buns.

Why are policewomen such great lovers?

They have big busts.

Why are chess players such great lovers?

They know how to mate.

Why are bartenders such adventurous lovers?

They do it with a blender.

UNSPEAKABLY GROSS JOKES

Why are debaters such lousy lovers?

They only do it orally.

Why are doctors such lousy lovers?

Because they always wait until the swelling goes down.

Why are kamikazes such lousy lovers?

They only do it once.

Why are musicians such lousy lovers?
They take notes.

Why are auctioneers such lousy lovers?
They talk while they do it.

Do old truckers ever die?
No, they just get new Petersbilt.

Do old fishermen ever die?
No, they just smell that way.

Do old math teachers ever die?

No, they just disintegrate.

Paratrooper: Dad, I did my first parachute jump today. I was too scared to jump at first, but the sergeant started yelling and cussing. Finally, since I hadn't moved an inch, he screamed at me, "Soldier, if you don't jump, I'm gonna screw you up the butt!"
Dad: And then you jumped?
Paratrooper: Just a little at first.

Chapter Seven:

Gross Elephant Jokes

What's gray and comes in quarts?

An elephant.

What's gray, fifteen feet long, and goes a hundred miles an hour?

An elephant dildo.

What should you do if you see an elephant coming through your window?

Swim.

What's the difference between a saloon and an elephant's fart?

A saloon is a barroom; an elephant's fart is a *BARROOOOOM!*

Have you heard about the elephant chiropractor?

He was an animal cracker.

What does an elephant use for a vibrator?
An epileptic.

What does an elephant use for a toothpick?
A Somali.

What does an elephant use for a tampon?
A sheep.

Did you hear about the elephant who died?

She got toxic sheep syndrome.

What's the difference between Louie Anderson and an elephant?

About ten pounds.

What's the black stuff between an elephant's toes?

Slow natives.

How can you tell that two elephants have been screwing in your backyard?

All the trash can liners are gone.

What did the elephant say to the naked man?

How do you breathe through that?

Then, what did the elephant say to the naked man?

That's cute, but does it pick up peanuts?

How do you make an elephant fly?

With a twelve-foot zipper.

How do you get an elephant into a phone booth?

With a chainsaw.

How do you get an elephant into a glove compartment?

With a blowtorch.

UNSPEAKABLY GROSS JOKES

Did you hear the one about the elephant with diarrhea?

I don't know why not, it was all over town.

What do you give an elephant with diarrhea?

A lot of room!

How can you tell if an elephant is on the rag?

You find a dime on your pillow, and your mattress is gone.

What should you do if you come across an elephant in the jungle?

Wipe it off.

How do you know an elephant's pecker is on his foot?

Because if he steps on you, you're fucked.

Chapter Eight:

Gross Gerbil Jokes

What goes *Thump-thump-thump, Thump-thump-thump*?

A three-legged gerbil on a wheel.

How many gerbils does it take to screw in a light bulb?

Two, only how do they get in there?

What's the quickest new way to get rich in America?

Gerbil breeding.

What does the new T-shirt from Greenpeace say?

"Save the gerbils! And if you don't know why, don't ask!"

Have you heard about the Rambo gerbil?

It goes in someone's butt and comes out with two of its buddies.

UNSPEAKABLY GROSS JOKES

What did one gerbil say to the other gerbil?

"Let's go to a gay bar and get shit-faced."

What did one gerbil say to the other gerbil when Bruce walked into the pet store?

"Quick, start barking!"

What did the brown gerbil at Bruce's house say to the white gerbil?

"You must be new here."

What did Bruce name his gerbils?

"Ooh" and "Aah."

How did Bruce know he was going to die in six weeks?

He saw a gerbil crawl out of his ass and see its shadow.

What does a gerbil do with his tail when he goes to bed?

Enjoys it.

Have you heard what's new about Vaseline?

Now the jar labels have pictures of missing gerbils.

Why did Bruce have to go to the hospital?

To have a mole removed.

UNSPEAKABLY GROSS JOKES

Why does Bruce wrap duct tape around his hamster?

So it won't explode when he fucks it.

Where did Richard Gere move after his gerbil operation?

To New Hamster.

A young boy went up to his father and said, "Can I have five bucks for a gerbil?"
His father said, "Here's twenty bucks. Get a hooker instead."

Chapter Nine:

Gross Animal Jokes

"Why do they call it an "orang-utang"?

Because of his two huge balls which bang together as he swings through the jungle: "a-RANG, a-TANG, a-RANG, a-TANG!"

Why don't chickens wear pants?

Because their peckers are on their faces.

How many animals are in a pair of pantyhose?

Fifteen: there's ten little piggies, two calves, an ass, a beaver, and a fish that no one's ever found.

What do you call a dog with no hind legs and steel balls?

Sparky.

What can you use a dog with no hind legs and steel balls for?

A wheelbarrow!

UNSPEAKABLY GROSS JOKES

What's the best thing about Dalmatians?

They make nice throw rugs.

What's the best thing about beagles?

Beagle burgers with cheese.

What do you call a dog skeleton that has been bleached white by the desert sun?

Milk Bones.

For dog lovers, what's the best way to start the day?

Beagle on a bagel for breakfast.

The sexual life of the camel is more than
  anyone thinks.
When the camel starts to get horny, he tries
  to mount the Sphinx.
But the Sphinx's celestial passage is blocked
  by the sands of the Nile.
That explains the hump on the camel, and
  the Sphinx's permanent smile.

Where do doggies go when they pass on?

Korean restaurants.

When you're camping, what do you get when you combine a dog, a long day of hiking, and a camp fire?

Spot chops.

When you're cooking dog, how do you know it's done?

It stops barking.

What's the difference between a man's pecker and a dog?

One tastes good with garlic.

What do you get when you combine a Korean chef and a poodle?

Dinner.

The bear went over the mountain,
To take a wee bit of a pee.
But fire flew out of his asshole
As far as the eye could see.

Where does virgin wool come from?

Ugly sheep.

What do you call a cat stuck in a meat grinder?

Meow Mix.

Where does the most accidental eating of pets occur?

In the home.

How do you make a cat sound like a dog?

Stick it in the corner, pour gasoline on it, light it, and "WHOOOOF!"

UNSPEAKABLY GROSS JOKES 91

Why is it important to keep your pet well groomed?

Everybody likes the meal to look good.

Why do mice have such small balls?

Hardly any of them know how to dance.

Mary had a little lamb.
The doctors were surprised.

Have you heard of the Ono Bird?

His legs are two inches long and his pecker is three inches long and every time he comes in for a landing he says, "Oh, no!!"

Why can't anyone catch a Gooney Bird?

When you chase him, he flies in smaller and smaller circles until he disappears up his own asshole.

I'm looking over my dead dog Rover
That I overlooked before.
One leg is severed, one leg is gone,
There's parts of him scattered all over the lawn.
No use explaining, the legs remaining
Are under the kitchen floor.
I'm looking over my dead dog Rover
That I overlooked before.

After you witness an animal get hit by a car, what is the first thing you should do?

Warm up the barbeque.

What do you call a horse that has reached the end of its productive life?

Alpo.

After witnessing a horse suffer a terrible accident, who is the first person you should call?

The purchasing agent from McDonald's.

What's the best thing to serve with horse steak?

Horse fries.

Once upon a time, there was a frog with a bright yellow pecker. The little frog was incredibly embarrassed by this, and went to ask Mother Nature to change his pecker into one more like a normal frog would have. When he got up to see Mother Nature, he told her how bad it was to have a bright yellow pecker, and asked her to please change it.

"I'm just Mother Nature," she told him. "The only miracle I perform is the miracle of life. If you have a personal request, you have to talk to God."

"How do I get to God?" asked the little frog.

"Just go right up that road."

The little frog began hopping away. Right behind him, in line to see Mother Nature, was a hippo with a bright blue nose. He told her how bad it was to have a bright blue nose, and asked her to please change it.

"I'm just Mother Nature," she said. "The only miracle I perform is the miracle of life. If you have a personal request, you have to talk to God."

"How do I get to God?"

"That's easy. Just follow the yellow-prick toad."

Chapter Ten:

Handy Bragging Tips for You and Your Friends

His cock was so big the whole town used it for a sundial.

Her breasts were so big she didn't need a life jacket.

His cock was so big it took him forty days to have one screw.

Her tits were so big she couldn't play golf—if she put the ball where she could see it, she couldn't hit it, and if she put the ball where she could hit it, she couldn't see it.

His cock was so long he didn't need a cane.

Her tits were so big that when she went swimming in the ocean the Iraqis took her for a two-headed torpedo.

His cock was so long that he couldn't see when he took a piss, but his neighbors could.

Her tits were so big she couldn't salute without bruising herself.

———————

His cock was so big it had its own address.

———————

Her crotch was so big it looked like an elephant's hips.

———————

His balls were so big that he used 'em for percussion.

———————

Her cunt-hole was so big it could hold groceries.

———————

He came in such quantities that the guy down the street started building a boat.

———————

She had gone down so much that she gargled with sperm.

———————

He farted so much that he got a job as a balloon inflator.

———————

Her ass was so tight it whistled in the wind.

———————

His breath was so bad it could knock a buzzard off a shit wagon.

———————

She kissed like the intake manifold of a diesel truck.

He was hornier than a double-dicked dog.

She was so flat she put her bra on backward and it fit.

He was so horny he had to have a cigarette after he stuffed the Thanksgiving turkey.

Her cunt-hole was smaller than a dimple.

He was so skinny that if he stuck out his tongue and stood sideways he looked like a zipper.

She was so wrinkled her face could hold a three-day rain.

He kissed worse than a Pez dispenser.

She was so ugly, her face was covered with pock marks from being touched with ten-foot poles.

He got more ass than a toilet seat.

Chapter Eleven:

Boogers, Farts, & More

What's this? [puff out your cheeks]

A dumb blonde's sperm bank.

Why shouldn't you throw toothpicks in a toilet?

Crabs can pole vault.

Why did they have to keep the heat turned up in Hitler's bunker?

So the lamp shades wouldn't get goose bumps.

Did you hear about the tall man who got fired?

He was sticking his business in everyone's nose.

How does a school cafeteria make a hamburger?

It sticks a pair of buns under a pig's nose and asks him to sneeze.

What's worse than shitting in the woods and using poison ivy for toilet paper?

Shitting over a bear trap and losing your ass.

How do you tell whether you should wear a sweatshirt or a windbreaker?

Well, that depends on whether you want to sweat or break wind.

"How Cold Is It?"
It's colder than the frost on a champagne glass;
It's colder than the pimple on a polar bear's ass;
It's colder than the nipple on a witch's tit;
It's colder than a bucket of penguin shit.

Why did God give Mexicans noses?

So they'd have something to pick in the off-season.

How do you recondition a stretched-out cunt-hole?

Stick a five-pound ham in it and pull out the bone.

Mahaffey was famous for his ability to eat just about any disgusting thing his buddies could think up. There wasn't a person in town who hadn't seen him eat a live goldfish, a cockroach, a ladle full of worms, or some equally sick thing.

One night at the bar, Mahaffey's buddies bet him he wouldn't drink the contents of the tavern spittoon. Mahaffey thought nothing of the challenge. He grasped the slimy cuspidor with both hands, threw his head back, and began to drink.

After about five seconds, the patrons at the bar began to applaud. Mahaffey had won the bet. But he kept drinking. The spectators started shouting, "Hey! Stop! You won! You won! STOP!!" But Mahaffey kept going until he had finished off the entire contents of the spittoon.

When he had swallowed the last drop, he set the container down on the bar. "Why didn't you stop?" gasped the customers. "Why didn't you stop?"

"I couldn't," said Mahaffey. "It was all one piece!"

Why is masturbation better than sex?

You can see what you're doing.

There once was a nympho named Alice
Who used a dynamite stick as a phallus.
They found her vagina
In North Carolina,
And her asshole in Buckingham Palace.

What's the difference between boogers and broccoli?

Kids won't eat broccoli.

———

Did you hear about the girl who used to take off her panties before she ate?

She wanted to keep the flies away from her food.

———

"Gross Camping Song"
Great green gobs of greasy grimy gopher guts,
Baked Alaskan gerbil butts, marmalade and auto nuts,
Mutilated monkey meat, little birdies' bloody feet,
And I forgot my spoon.
Chopped-up baby parakeets, green maggot pie,
Three dog's livers and one cat's eye,
A squirrel-shit sandwich, layered on thick,
Oh, what a tasty stew.

———

How do you play Switch?

You put one thumb in your mouth and one thumb up your butt, and every ten seconds you switch.

Is Tampax the best thing on earth?

No, but it's next to the best.

What is a used tampon good for?

A vampire tea bag.

Did you hear about the obnoxious guy who insulted the waitress and then ordered a Bloody Mary?

She brought him his drink with the string still in it.

What would John F. Kennedy be doing if he were alive today?

Scratching on the inside of his coffin.

A dead man was brought into the emergency room at a large hospital. The doctor could tell by the odor that alcohol had been involved. The man's friend was with him, completely sober, and not very shook up.

"Excuse me, sir," said the doctor. "Can you tell me anything about how this man died?"

"He was happy right to the end. He drowned in a vat of beer."

"How long was he in there until you found him?"

"Oh, we finally got him out after about four hours."

"It took you four hours to get him out?"

"That's right. You see, every time we got him out, he took a leak and dove back in."

Why did the hungry idiot start to cry?

He had just blown his nose and threw away the tissue.

Why didn't the guy pull the hair out of his food?

He didn't mind eating pubies.

What's green and runs from bed to bed?

Lizard Taylor.

What's green and flies over Germany?

Snotsies.

What's green and flies over Russia?

Peter Panov.

What's brown and full of holes?

Swiss shit.

What's brown and sounds like a bell?

Dung.

How can you tell if your date has been waiting for you for a long time?

He's standing in a puddle.

Why are computer chips so small?

Computers don't eat much.

Have you heard about the new how-to book on oral sex?

It's called *Vacuum Lips* by Dewey Suk and Jesse Du.

There once was a woman named Lynn,
Whose mother, to save her from sin,
Took some shellac
And filled up her crack,
But the boys picked it out with a pin.

Have you heard about the dirty old lady's pet cat?

It died of a pubic hairball.

Why did seventy whales beach themselves in Mexico?

They thought it was Waco, Texas.

What do you call three Broadway singers on fire?

A torch song trilogy.

What do you call a cop car on fire?

A pig roast.

Why do poor people wear pointed shoes?

To kill cockroaches in the corner.

Grandma's in the kitchen, fixing up the batter,
Making pancakes on the dirty, grimy floor.
Her eyes are filled with matter, and it's dripping in the batter,
And the snot keeps a-running from her nose.

Two guys are eating pizza in a restaurant. The first guy says, "This pizza sucks. I'd rather fuck the pizza and eat the waitress."

The second guy says, "I did already. The pizza's better."

"Mommy, Mommy, Daddy's heaving his cookies in the bathroom!"

"So, what's the matter, dear?"

"Sister's getting all the big chunks."

"Mommy, Mommy, can I borrow your curling iron?"

"What for, dear?"

"We're playing Spanish Inquisition with little Suzie."

"Mommy, what's for dinner?"
"Shut up and get back in the oven."

Teacher: Carla, what does your father do for a living?
Carla: My father's dead.
Teacher: What did he do before he died?
Carla: He went, "AAAAUUGH!!"

A man went to see his doctor with a strange problem. It seemed that every time he farted, it made the sound "HONDA!"

The doctor gave him every test he could think of and found nothing wrong. He then looked through all the medical journals, consulted all the specialists, and still could find no precedent for the man's condition. At long last, he had an idea. "It's a long shot," he said, "but if your farts go 'HONDA,' then maybe a Honda expert can help you."

The doctor placed a long-distance call to the Honda factory in Japan. When he explained the situation, the factory doctor was put on the phone.

"Hello, I have a patient here that has a unique problem. When he experiences flatulence, it makes the sound 'HONDA.' Is there anything you can tell me about this?"

The Japanese doctor said, "See if the patient has an abscess."

The doctor fixed the man up with a dentist, who found an abscessed tooth. After a short treatment with antibiotics, both the abscess and the farting problem were gone.

The man was amazed. "I can't thank you enough, Doc! How did you do it?"

The doctor himself didn't know how. He decided to call the Japanese doctor and find out. "Hello, I want to thank you. You diagnosed and cured my patient from ten thousand miles away. How did you do it?"

"Very simple," said the Japanese doctor. "Abscess makes the fart go 'HONDA.'"

Two hobos were walking down the road. They hadn't eaten in two days. They came upon a dead raccoon run over in the road. "Pete," said the first hobo, "I'm so hungry, I'm gonna eat that raccoon. Do you want any?"

"No thanks, Worzel," said the second hobo. "I think I'll wait."

Worzel ate the raccoon, and they kept walking. Soon they came upon a dead squirrel run over in the road. "Pete," said Worzel,

"I'm still hungry. I'm gonna eat that squirrel. Do you want any?"

"No thanks, I think I'll wait."

Worzel ate the squirrel, and they kept walking. Along the way they saw a few dead birds, a dead frog, and a few dead bugs stuck to a windshield. Worzel ate them all. All of a sudden, Worzel heaved a steaming pile of puke on the side of the road.

"Just what I've been waiting for," cried Pete. "A nice hot meal!"

Chapter Twelve:

Watch Your Fucking Language

What do you call a woman who insists on remaining a virgin?

In-"F"-able.

What did the husband say when his wife lectured him on using profanity?

"If they can say 'intercourse' on TV, then I can surely say 'fuck' in my own home!"

If the thing between a woman's legs is her vulva, then what's a cunt?

The rest of her.

What do you call a female clone?

A clunt.

How can you ruin someone's reputation and not be sued for libel?

Tell everyone you saw them masticating in public.

UNSPEAKABLY GROSS JOKES

A proper young lady bought a parrot. When she got the parrot home, the bird took one look around and said, "God damn, what the hell's going on around here?"

The woman was shocked. "Now, listen, Mr. Parrot, I don't want to hear that kind of language again. Do you understand?"

The parrot said, "God damn, what the hell's going on around here?"

The young lady was extremely perturbed. She said, "Listen to me carefully. I don't want to hear you speak in that manner. Got it?"

The parrot said, "God damn, what the hell's going on around here?"

At her wits' end, the woman tried to reason with the creature one more time. "Listen to me, you filthy bird, if you say anything like that again, I'll . . . I'll put you in the freezer!"

The parrot said, "God damn, what the hell's going on around here?"

The woman grabbed the parrot by his feet and slammed him into the freezer. The parrot was taken by surprise. There he was in the freezer. After he collected himself, he glanced around and noticed a frozen chicken.

"Holy shit!" the parrot gasped. "What did *you* say? Fuck?"

What do you call four black dudes in a Chevy?

A blood vessel.

What did Little Red Riding Hood say when the wolf threatened to eat her?

"Eat, eat, eat. Doesn't anyone fuck anymore?"

What did the foul-mouthed, street-smart, low-life criminal say after he got a lesson in proper speech habits?

"I took the fuckin' broad to the fuckin' motel and we had some fuckin' drinks. Then we enjoyed a period of intercourse."

What do you call a woman without an asshole?

Divorced.

Why did God put cunts on women?

So men would talk to them.

What do you say to someone who's into necrophilia, bestiality, and sadism?

"I think you're beating a dead horse."

How do you get three little old ladies to say, "Fuck!"?

Have another little old lady shout, "Bingo!"

Why didn't the prudish editor put dashes in place of offensive words?

He only had his asterisk.

She was riding down the highway doin'
   ninety miles an hour
When the chain on her motorcycle broke.
Well, they found her in the grass
With the muffler up her ass
And her titties playing "Dixie" on the
   spokes.

Now that there's sex ed, what do the kids learn in school?

Reading, writing, and a rhythmic dick.

What did the teenager say when he flunked sex ed?

"That fucking teacher! I'm gonna kick her in the balls!"

Did you hear about the word expert whose friend came to him looking for sympathy?

He told her she could find it between sodomy and syphilis . . . in the dictionary.

What should you do during National Cunnilingus Week?

Take a clitoris to lunch.

What happened to the fly on the toilet seat?

He regularly got pissed off.

Why was the bathroom at the radiator shop always so busy?

Because their ads said it was the best place to take a leak.

Did you hear about the fool who was called a goddamned, cocksucking, baby-raping, masturbating, motherfucking son of a bitch?

He said, "I *am not* a masturbator!"

Why did the chicken cross the basketball court?

He heard the referee was blowing fouls.

What's a virgin?

Someone who doesn't give a fuck.

Why did so many black soldiers die in Vietnam?

Because if someone shouted, "Get down!" they all got up and danced.

Why did the little penguin ask her parents whether they were both purebred penguins?

Because she was fuckin' freezing!

What did the Chinese man say to the political candidate?

"Rotsa ruck with your erection!"

What should you do if you have a mosquito on your prick?

Beat it off!

One day, little Billy's mother was tired of Billy's constant chatter, so she told him to go across the street to watch the construction workers so he could learn something. After two hours, he came back in the house, and his mother said, "What did you learn?"

"Well, first you take a goddamned door and try to fit it into the fucking doorway. If the sonovabitch don't fit, then you take the cocksucker down, shave a cunt-hair off it, and put the motherfucker back up again."

Billy's mother was absolutely shocked. She told him, "You just wait until your father gets home—you're in big trouble!"

When Billy's father came home, Mother said to Billy, "Now, I want you to tell your father what you learned across the street."

Billy repeated the whole story. His father was furious. He said, "Billy, go outside and get me a switch!"

"Fuck you!" said Billy. "That's the fucking electrician's job!"

Chapter Thirteen:

What Movie Ratings Really Mean

rating	what it means to the movie industry	what it means to old people	what it really means
G	General audiences	Good	for Girls only
PG-13	Parental Guidance suggested for children under 13	Pretty Good	Pukey Gunk; wouldn't see it for 13¢
PG	Parental Guidance suggested	still Pretty Good	Pathetic Garbage
R	Restricted; no unaccompanied minors	Rotten	Right on!
NC-17	No Children under 17	Not Comfortable	Nice Cunts!
XXX	Dirty Dirty Dirty!	Heck No!	X-cellent!

Chapter Fourteen:

AIDS Jokes

How can you tell if your garden has AIDS?
Your pansies are dying.

How did the minister get AIDS?
He didn't clean his organ between hymns.

What's the difference between Rock Hudson and Saddam Hussein?

Saddam Hussein's aides haven't killed him yet.

What's the difference between Staten Island and Freddie Mercury?

Staten Island is a ferry terminal and Freddie is a terminal fairy.

Why did the porn star expose her tits at the AIDS benefit?

Because the crowd was shouting, "A cure or bust," and she didn't have a cure.

Which of these things doesn't belong: AIDS, gonorrhea, cancer, condominium?

Gonorrhea. You *can* get rid of it.

Why are researchers having such a hard time finding a cure for AIDS?

They can't get their lab mice to buttfuck.

Chapter Fifteen:

Somalia

How many Somalis can you get in a phone booth?

All of them.

What's black, round, and covered with cobwebs?

A Somali's asshole.

What's the main reason for a child's disappearance in Somalia?

The wind.

What do you call a Somali wearing a turban?

A Q-tip.

What do you call a Somali with a dime on his head?

A nail.

What do you call a Somali with a Mohawk hairdo?

A toothbrush.

What do you call a Somali with a swollen foot?

A three wood.

What do you call a Somali with buck teeth?

A rake.

What special feature does the McDonald's in Somalia have?

A crawl-up window.

What has five million legs and weighs thirty pounds?

The entire population of Somalia.

Why can't a Somali go to a movie theatre?
He can't keep the seat down.

———————

Whose measurements are 10-5-10?
Miss Somalia.

———————

How can you tell if a Somali is pregnant?
Hold her up to the light.

———————

What can a Somali do with a key ring?
Use it for a belt.

———————

What do Somalis use Venetian blinds for?

Bunk beds.

How do you start a fire?

Rub two Somalis together.

What's another way to describe a Uniform Price Code scanning bar?

A family portrait of Somalis.

Chapter Sixteen:

"Shitty" Jokes

How do we know that eating shit is good for us?

A million flies can't be wrong.

Why is it a good idea not to flush the toilet?

The next guy might be hungry.

What should you do if you're making a pie and your cat takes a shit in the filling?

Stir vigorously!

How dry I am, how wet I'll be,
If I don't find the bathroom key.

Did you hear about the black youngster who started to cry when he got diarrhea?

He thought he was melting.

What do you call a house made out of shit?

A log cabin.

UNSPEAKABLY GROSS JOKES

What's grosser than taking a shit in the shower?

Trying to stomp it down the drain.

Mary had a little watch,
She swallowed it one day,
And now she's taking laxatives
To pass the time away.
But as the days went on and on
The watch refused to pass.
So if you want to know the time,
Just look up Mary's ass.

A man went to see his doctor. He told him he was having trouble with his bowels. The doctor asked him, "Do you have regular bowel movements?"

"Yes," the man said, "every morning at seven A.M."

"Well, then, what's the problem?"

"I don't get up until ten o'clock."

Did you hear that diarrhea is hereditary?

It "runs" in the family.

Just when I thought I had some sense,
I stuck my dick in an electric fence.
All the hair burned off my balls,
Then I shit in my overalls.

A little boy's father had just died. His friend asked him, "What did your father die of?"
"Gonorrhea."
"That's not what I heard," said his friend. "I heard he died of diarrhea."
"Listen here," said the boy, "my dad was a fuckin' man, not a shit-ass."

Chapter Seventeen:

Tongue Twisters

Show me the chair Schmidt sat in when he was shot.

———————

The sinking steamer sunk. (Repeat five times without pause)

———————

Sally sat and shivered. (Repeat five times without pause)

———————

I slit a sheet, a sheet I slit.
Upon the slitted sheet I sit.

———————

Six sick sucks under six slick sheets.

———————

How many sheets could a sheet-slinger
 sling
If a sheet-slinger could sling sheets?

———————

Charlotte shuns sunshine; Sarah shuns sleet.

———————

How many figs would a fig-plucker pluck
If a fig-plucker could pluck figs?

———————

UNSPEAKABLY GROSS JOKES

Who was the city guy who shot the city sheriff?

One smart fella, he felt smart.
Two smart fellas, they *both* felt smart.
Three smart fellas, they *all* felt smart.

Peter Piper pricked his pecker picking prickly peppers.

Chapter Eighteen:

Sexual Specialties

What's twelve inches long and white?

Nothing!

What happens when an Italian with a hard-on runs into a wall?

He breaks his nose.

Which came first, the chicken or the egg?

Neither. The rooster came first.

A young man went up to his father and asked him, "Can I have twenty bucks for a blow job?"
His father said, "I don't know. Are you any good?"

What sign did the masochist wear?

"Please spindle, fold, or mutilate."

Do you know what mothballs smell like?

How did you get their legs apart?

What's the quickest way to circumcise someone?

Put broken glass in his friend's butt.

How do you explain physics to a sex-hungry idiot?

Tell him, "The heat of the meat plus the mass of the ass equals the angle of the dangle."

What do dildos and soybeans have in common?

They're both meat substitutes.

What do you do with a woman who drinks?

Liquor.

Did you hear about the rich WASP who, after twenty years, finally made his wife happy?

He bought her a lesbian.

Why did the lumber truck stop?

To let the lumber jack off.

Why is sex like a snowfall?

You're never sure how many inches you'll get.

What did the woman say to her swimming instructor?

"Will I really drown if you take your finger out?"

What did one testicle say to the other?

Don't mind that asshole behind you. We're working for the prick up front.

What do you call a shipment of vibrators?

Toys for twats.

A woman went into a fine department store and asked to see a pair of brown gloves. The clerk began asking detailed questions about how long she wanted the gloves to be, what type of material, what shade of brown is her coat, and on and on. Finally, she could stand it no longer. "Listen, you idiot, the gloves don't have to match my coat. They're for finger-fucking only!"

Percy: Would you like some canned nuts?
Farrah: Gee, I've never had it in THAT far.

What's a necrophiliac's biggest complaint about sex?

They just kinda lay there.

UNSPEAKABLY GROSS JOKES

What's a necrophiliac's favorite movie?

Night of the Living Dead.

Where does a necrophiliac go to pick up women?

A funeral home.

What's red and has seven dents?

Snow White's cherry.

Why did the woman get thrown out of the riding stable?

She wanted to mount the horse *her* way.

What's the worst part of having a parquet floor?

Cleaning up the margarine afterward.

Reporter: Are you bisexual?

Model: Hell no— I've never had to buy it.

Client: Are you into domination?

Call Girl: No— I'm not very religious.

What is skinny-dipping?

Fucking a man with a pindick.

What's a wet dream?

Sex in the shower.

What should you do if you're feeling down?

Insert your finger.

Why did the dominatrix fire her broker?

He bought her some bonds, but they weren't any fun at all.

Why is a good orgy like a house?

The studs are just sixteen inches apart.

What did one man say to the other man in the same bed?

"This wife-swapping was a good idea. I only hope our wives are hitting it off."

What did the sadist do when the masochist said, "Hurt me"?

She said, "No."

A woman contacted the spirit of her dead husband during a seance. "How are things on the other side?" she said.
"Oh, just great. I eat ten times a day, and I fuck fifty times a day."
"Are you in heaven?"
"No, I'm a rabbit in Arizona."